101 WAYS TO KILL YOUR BOSS

GRAHAM ROUMIEU

headline

First published in 2007
by HEADLINE PUBLISHING GROUP

First published in paperback in 2008
by HEADLINE PUBLISHING GROUP

1

Cataloguing in Publication Data is available from the
British Library

ISBN 978 0 7553 4236 5

Typeset by Avon DataSet Ltd, Bidford-on-Avon,
Warwickshire

Printed in the UK by
CPI William Clowes Beccles NR34 7TL

Headline's policy is to use papers that are natural, renew-
able and recyclable products and made from wood
grown in sustainable forests. The logging and manufac-
turing processes are expected to conform to the environ-
mental regulations of the country of origin.

HEADLINE PUBLISHING GROUP
An Hachette Livre UK Company
338 Euston Road
London NW1 3BH

www.headline.co.uk
www.hachettelivre.co.uk

101 WAYS TO KILL YOUR BOSS

For Dad

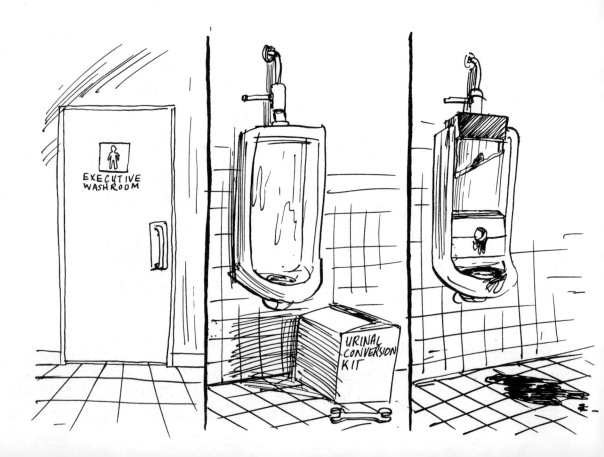

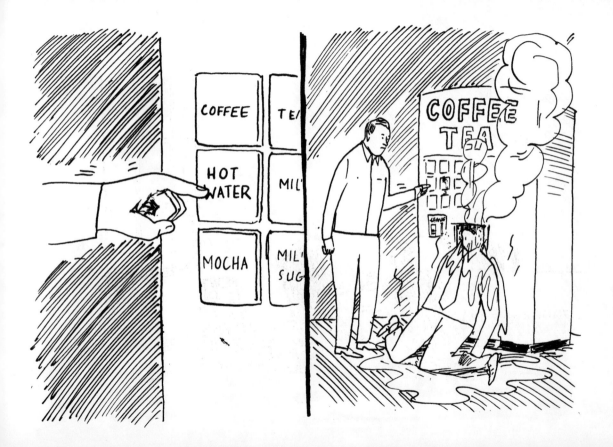

flick

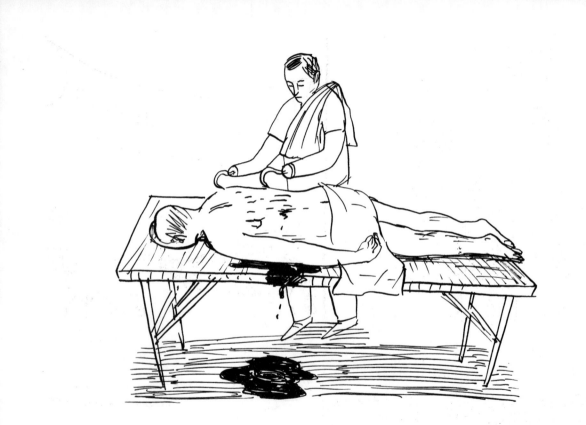

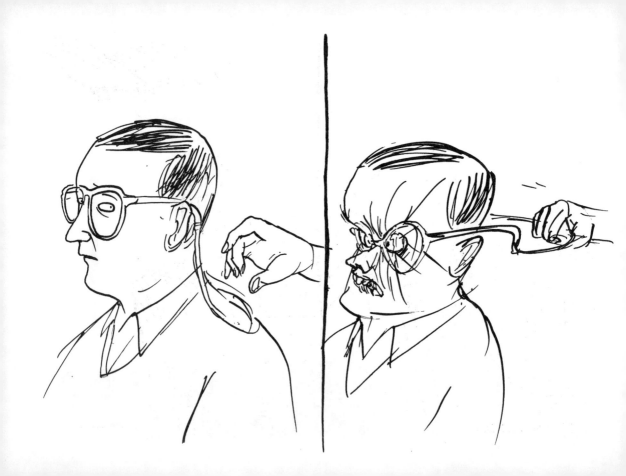

I HATE THIS GUY →

£7.99
Humour 978 0 7553 1804 9